WONDER WOMAN

❧ CONTAGION ❧

WONDER WOMAN

⊰ CONTAGION ⊱

Gail Simone
Writer

**Nicola Scott Aaron Lopresti Chris Batista
Fernando Dagnino Travis Moore**
Pencillers

**Doug Hazlewood Matt Ryan
Raul Fernandez Bit Wayne Faucher
Brad Anderson John Dell Hi-Fi**
Inkers

Brad Anderson Hi-Fi
Colorists

Travis Lanham
Letterer

Nicola Scott with Hi-Fi
Cover art

Wonder Woman created by William Moulton Marston

Brian Cunningham
Editor-original series

Sean Ryan
Associate Editor-original series

Bob Harras
Group Editor-Collected Editions

Anton Kawasaki
Editor

Robbin Brosterman
Design Director-Books

DC COMICS

Diane Nelson
President

Dan DiDio and Jim Lee
Co-Publishers

Geoff Johns
Chief Creative Officer

Patrick Caldon
EVP-Finance and Administration

John Rood
EVP-Sales, Marketing and
Business Development

Amy Genkins
SVP-Business and Legal Affairs

Steve Rotterdam
SVP-Sales and Marketing

John Cunningham
VP-Marketing

Terri Cunningham
VP-Managing Editor

Alison Gill
VP-Manufacturing

David Hyde
VP-Publicity

Sue Pohja
VP-Book Trade Sales

Alysse Soll
VP-Advertising and Custom
Publishing

Bob Wayne
VP-Sales

Mark Chiarello
Art Director

WONDER WOMAN:
CONTAGION

Published by DC Comics.
Cover and compilation
Copyright © 2010 DC Comics.
All Rights Reserved.

Originally published in single
magazine form in WONDER
WOMAN 40-44. Copyright
© 2010 DC Comics. All Rights
Reserved. All characters, their
distinctive likenesses and
related elements featured in
this publication are trademarks
of DC Comics. The stories,
characters and incidents
featured in this publication
are entirely fictional.
DC Comics does not read or
accept unsolicited submissions
of ideas, stories or artwork.

DC Comics, 1700 Broadway,
New York, NY 10019
A Warner Bros. Entertainment
Company
Printed by Quad/Graphics,
Dubuque, IA, USA. 9/15/10.
First printing.
ISBN: 978-1-4012-2920-7

A MURDER OF CROWS
PART ONE

HIT THE GROUND RUNNING

Aaron Lopresti Penciller
Matt Ryan Inker

Cover by Aaron Lopresti

MY TWO PEOPLE ARE NOT THAT DIFFERENT.

ABOVE, A SHINING CITY OF LIFE AND FUNCTION.

WHILE ANOTHER WORLD OF TUNNELS AND ALCOVES EXISTS IN THE UNDERWORLD, MAKING PERFECT HOMES FOR VERMIN AND THE FORGOTTEN.

AND SOMETHING ELSE, OF LATE.

SNFF

THIRTY MINUTES AGO, SOMETHING DEVOURED AN ENTIRE METRO SUBWAY TRAIN IN THIS EXACT TUNNEL.

AND IT LOOKS LIKE WHATEVER HAD THAT MEAL HAS COME BACK.

SERPENTS.

THEY NEVER LEARN ABOUT PORTION CONTROL.

FOR A LONG TIME, THE LIGHTS OF THE MODERN LIFE KEPT THE DARK OF LEGEND AT BAY.

THOSE UNDERWORLDERS AND THE GODS THAT SPAWNED THEM WERE BAFFLED AND REPELLED BY THE MACHINES AND TECHNOLOGY OF THIS WORLD.

SOMETHING'S HAPPENING.

A TINY MORSSSEL, BUT ONE I CONSSSUME WITH ENTHUSSSIASSM, PRINCESS OF PREY.

REALLY.

HOW FLATTERING.

AND OF COURSE, A METRO TRAIN IS COMING RIGHT FOR US.

PERHAPS THE PLUMED SERPENT HAS BARBECUE FOR ITS SUPPER.

HOOONNKK

KRRACKK

THEN AGAIN...

...PERHAPS NOT.

YOU HAVE TAKEN MY FANGS! YOU HAVE CASTRATED ME.

NOT YET. BUT I'M CONSIDERING.

DO YOU BELIEVE YOU HAVE BEATEN QUETZLOTL?

SCION OF THE EARTH AND BROTHER OF THE WIND?

I, WHO COUNT THE ELEMENTS AS MY SERVANTS?

SERPENTS NEVER STOP BOASTING, EITHER.

THOOM

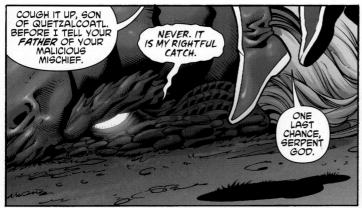

COUGH IT UP, SON OF *QUETZALCOATL*. BEFORE I TELL YOUR *FATHER* OF YOUR MALICIOUS MISCHIEF.

NEVER. IT IS MY *RIGHTFUL CATCH*.

ONE LAST CHANCE, SERPENT GOD.

OR ELSE I'LL TAKE THE REST OF YOUR TEETH AND YOU CAN *GUM* YOUR MEALS FOR THE NEXT FEW CENTURIES, AND THEN... AND *THEN*, SNAKE LORD...

...THEN I'LL START TAKING THINGS FROM YOU THAT YOU'LL *REALLY* MISS.

CURSE YOU, YOU AND ALL YOUR KIND.

AKCKCKCKCKK...

EXCUSE ME.

I KNOW THIS GOD. HE HAS NEVER BEEN... A *CONSUMER* OF HUMAN FLESH BEFORE. HE'D RATHER GET *PRAISE* FROM PEOPLE THAN BE *SATED* BY THEM.

WHY IS HE *HERE*?

NO ONE SEEMS BADLY INJURED, BLESS THE GODS.

IS EVERYONE ALL RIGHT?

YOU'RE SAFE NOW, EVERYONE. PLEASE EXIT CAREFULLY.

PRINCESS... WONDER WOM... I DON'T KNOW WHAT TO CALL YOU.

DIANA IS FINE, SISTER.

WATCH YOUR STEP, PLEASE.

MY CHILDREN WANTED TO *THANK* YOU.

WE GOT *EATED* BY A *SNAKE*!

CHILDREN. SUCH A GLORIOUS PHENOMENON.

YOU'RE SO PRETTY. I GOT YOUR LUNCH BOX.

WHO CARES ABOUT *THAT?* SHE'S *TOUGH.*

THANK YOU, CHILDREN. I THINK YOU'RE BOTH VERY BRAVE.

GOOD FORTUNE SMILE UPON YOU ALL.

I ADMIRE THEIR OPTIMISM.

WHY DOES THE LOSS OF THAT QUALITY SOMEHOW CONSTITUTE WISDOM, IN OUR PERCEPTION?

SHE SAVED THEM ALL.

A TRUE HERO.

IT'S INSPIRING.

ARE YOU INJURED, LORD OF SERPENTS?

...NO.

I DO NOT KNOW WHY MY APPETITE... I DO NOT KNOW WHY I DID THISSSS.

I USUALLY LOATHE THE TASSSTE OF HUMAN FLESH!

DO YOU NEED ANY HELP GETTING HOME?

NOT AS LONG AS THERE ARE CLOUDSSS IN THE SSSKY.

I AM SSSORRY, PRINCESSS.

SSSSOMETHING CALLED ME HERE.

MADE ME BLIND WITH HUNGER.

I FEAR MORE WILL COME, AND THEY TOO WILL WISSSH TO FEED.

BE WARY, PRINCESSS.

EVEN NOW, YOUR CITY SSMELLSS LIKE A SSLAUGHTER-HOUSSE.

I FIND WHEN A SERPENT GOD BOTHERS TO GIVE YOU A WARNING LIKE THAT...

...IT IS ONLY PRUDENT TO TAKE *HEED.*

HM. NOTHING FOR IT, I SUPPOSE.

UNFORTUNATELY, FIRST...

...I SUPPOSE IT'S LEFT TO *ME* TO DO THE *DISHES.*

I'M EVER SO PLEASED THAT YOU ARE SAFE FROM THAT HORRIBLE CREATURE.

WONDER WOMAN *SAVED* US.

SHE CERTAINLY DID, ONLY...

...WELL, IT'S JUST THAT, AND I HESITATE TO BRING IT UP, BUT...

DID SHE *HAVE* TO DESTROY THIS LOVELY PARK?

AND DIDN'T SHE ENDANGER YOU ALL BY SO CARELESSLY FIGHTING THAT LARGE SNAKE?

WHAT ARE YOU SAYING? SHE RISKED HER *LIFE.*

YES, SHE DID, AND BLESS HER FOR THAT SELFLESS ACT. STILL...

...MAYBE SHE ONLY WANTS THE GLORY?

I WONDER. SHE SEEMED AWFULLY *CHUMMY* WITH THE SNAKE JUST NOW.

OH, YES, *EVER SO* CHUMMY!

YOU DON'T SUPPOSE, I MEAN, YOU DON'T THINK THEY COULD HAVE *CONSPIRED* TO DO THIS? FOR THE *ATTENTION,* I MEAN?

HEAVENS, WHAT A HORRENDOUS *THOUGHT!*

NOT *DIANA!* NEVER *DIANA!*

I'M *CERTAIN* YOU'RE RIGHT, SCORPION. I DON'T KNOW WHAT I WAS THINKING.

A VERY GOOD EVENING TO YOU, MA'AM. SORRY TO HAVE TROUBLED YOU.

MOM. SHE SAVED US, DIDN'T SHE?

I...

I DON'T KNOW, TRAVIS.

SHOCKING, HOW PEOPLE TURN ON THEIR HEROES, THESE DAYS. ANYTHING *GOOD* IN THERE, ADDER?

I SHOULD SAY NOT, GOAT. CELERY STICKS AND MILK. P.B.&J. HMM.

I *HAD* HOPED FOR BLOOD.

RATHER HAD MY HEART *SET*, IN FACT.

MY FRIEND. MY NON-AMAZON SISTER.

HERE BECAUSE OF HER CONNECTION TO ME.

I LOVE YOU, ETTA. I LOVE WHAT YOU REPRESENT IN THE OUTSIDE WORLD.

PLEASE BE WELL.

I MISSED YOU TERRIBLY.

CAN YOU EVER FORGIVE ME?

DIANA!

I MISSED YOU. YOU OKAY?

AM I OKAY.

YES.

NOW I AM.

IS SHE SUPPOSED TO BE STANDING UP LIKE THIS, DIRECTOR TREVOR?

NO OFFENSE, DIANA, BUT EVEN YOU CAN'T MAKE HER DO ANYTHING SHE DOESN'T WANT TO.

AND YOU LOVE ME FOR IT!

I DO. I ABSOLUTELY DO.

I BROUGHT YOU THESE WARRIOR BLOSSOMS FROM THEMYSCIRA.

IT'S BEST TO KEEP SMALL PETS AWAY FROM THEM. AND CHILDREN.

OH. OKAY. THANKS. THAT'S REALLY NICE OF YOU.

...A *DOUBLE* TRAGEDY AS A RESPECTED LOCAL LAWYER WAS APPARENTLY ROBBED AND SHOT TO DEATH EVEN AS A LONG-CHERISHED SYNAGOGUE WAS GOING UP IN FLAMES IN THIS NORMALLY QUIET WASHINGTON NEIGHBORHOOD.

THIS IS TANSIE CHEN SPEAKING *EXCLUSIVELY* WITH A YOUNG MAN WHO CLAIMS TO HAVE *WITNESSED* THE TRAGEDY.

GOSH, YES. IT WAS AWFUL!

WE *ALL* SAW IT!

I KNOW THIS IS PAINFUL, BUT CAN YOU DESCRIBE THE MAN WHO...

YES. HE WAS A BIG *BLACK* MAN.

AND HE KEPT SHOUTING THE MOST *AWFUL* THINGS ABOUT WHITE PEOPLE.

WE'RE GONNA LOSE THE BUILDING, CHIEF.

CAPTAIN JOHN F.D. McRAE

I KNOW THAT, SIMS. LET'S MAKE SURE WE DON'T LOSE THE REST OF THE BLOCK, ALL RIGHT?

DAMN. HOW'D IT GET OUT OF CONTROL SO *FAST?*

THAT'S A QUESTION I FIND MYSELF ASKING ALL THE *TIME.*

I'VE BEEN A CHECKMATE OPERATIVE UNDER U.N. AUTHORITY FOR THE LAST THREE YEARS.

MY JOB WAS TO OBSERVE ANOMALIES IN THE DAY-TO-DAY OPERATIONS OF THE D.M.A. AND REPORT BACK TO HEADQUARTERS IN THE SWISS ALPS.

ETTA OLIVE CANDY
OPERATIVE LEVEL: KNIGHT
SPECIAL LIAISON
SECURITY COLOR: WHITESIDE

HOLD ON. WAIT.

WHAT?

"RECRUITED IN THE MIDDLE OF THE NIGHT, BY GREEN LANTERN AND MR. TERRIFIC THEMSELVES.

"THEY HAVE OPERATIVES EVERYWHERE, DIANA. 'PAWNS,' THEY CALL THEM.

YOUR WORK WITH THE USAF IS IMPORTANT, MISS CANDY. WE RECOGNIZE THAT.

BUT WE'RE OFFERING YOU A CHANCE TO CHANGE THE *WORLD.*

"YOU HAVE TO UNDERSTAND. I WAS *PROUD* TO BE AIR FORCE."

BUT WHEN YOUR HUSBAND IS THE DEPUTY SECRETARY OF DEFENSE, AND YOUR BEST FRIEND IS AN AMAZON WARRIOR PRINCESS, WELL...

...IT CAN MAKE YOU FEEL A LITTLE INADEQUATE, YOU KNOW?

SWEETHEART--

I'M NOT *BLAMING* ANYONE, STEVE.

"BUT WHEN THEY OFFERED ME A CHANCE TO BE IMPORTANT...A CHANCE TO MATTER...

"...I PUT AWAY THE PERSON I HAD BECOME AND TOOK IT.

"THEY WERE READY TO DROP ME STRAIGHT INTO A DIPLOMATIC POSITION, BUT I ASKED FOR FIELD WORK, FIRST.

"INSISTED ON TAKING THE FULL PHYSICAL TRAINING REGIMEN. IT AIN'T NAVY SEALS, BUT IT'S NO AFTERNOON TAI CHI SESSION, EITHER. DROPPED FIFTY POUNDS, I HASTEN TO ADD.

"I LIKED IT, DIANA. AND THIS MAY BE HARD TO BELIEVE--

"--BUT I WAS GOOD AT IT.

I DON'T FIND THAT HARD TO BELIEVE AT ALL. I KNEW YOU WERE *ALWAYS* FORMIDABLE.

WELL, THAT MAKES ONE OF US. BUT I ASKED TO BE IN THE ACTION, DIANA. I WANTED...

HAVE A GOOD HOLIDAY GUY TOM

"...I DON'T KNOW WHAT I WANTED.

"BUT I FOUND SOMETHING.

"TRIAL BY FIRE, I GUESS. YOU'D KNOW MORE ABOUT THIS THAN ME."

WE AMAZONS CALL IT "SLEEPING NEXT TO SCORPIONS."

BY FACING YOUR FEAR, YOU LEARN TO...

...TO CONTROL IT. YES. EXACTLY.

"I TOOK THOSE CHALLENGES MYSELF, ETTA. WITHOUT CHAPERONES OR PERMISSION.

"MY MOTHER WAS FURIOUS."

HEH. BET *THAT* WAS SOMETHING TO SEE.

BUT THAT'S NOT THE POINT, DIANA. THE *POINT*...

...IS THAT I *ASKED* FOR THIS LIFE. AND I *LOVE* IT.

GENOCIDE OR NO, HOSPITAL OR NO.

IT WAS *MY* DECISIONS THAT PUT ME HERE.

AND I'M NOT GOING TO HAVE YOU LOOKING AT ME WITH GUILTY, MOPEY EYES EVERY TIME YOU LOOK AT ME.

YOU DIDN'T DO THIS.

GENOCIDE DID.

ETTA, I HAVE TO...

SWEETIE, JUST GO. YOU WERE GIVEN ALL THAT POWER FOR A *REASON*, WEREN'T YOU?

*B*LESS MY FRIEND, ATHENA. THE KNACK OF KNOWING JUST THE RIGHT THING TO SAY IS RARE AND A LITTLE BIT INVALUABLE.

FORMIDABLE, INDEED.

WHERE TO START?

THE FIRES DON'T SEEM DIRECTED AT THE SEAT OF GOVERNMENT...

UNLESS I'M MISTAKEN, THE BIGGEST FIRE IS AT THE CENTER OF THE CITY ALMOST *EXACTLY.*

THAT INDICATES *PLANNING.*

WAIT.

I KNOW THAT SOUND.

A MURDER OF CROWS

PART TWO

THROWDOWN

Chris Batista and Fernando Dagnino Pencillers
Doug Hazlewood and Raul Fernandez Inkers

Cover by Aaron Lopresti

THALARION.

IN THE SHORT TIME SINCE MY REBIRTH I HAVE NOT SPENT A SINGLE SLUMBER ON THIS ISLAND.

MY KINGDOM. MY ISLAND.

MY CITY OF CRYSTAL.

JASON AND HIS CREW WERE MEN OF ACTION IN THEIR PREVIOUS LIVES. THEY LOOK TO ME FOR ANSWERS.

AND WISDOM, NEVER MY STRONG SUIT AT THE BEST OF TIMES.

AND I AM LONELY. THEY DO NOT UNDERSTAND ME, AND I DO NOT UNDERSTAND THE WORLD BEYOND THESE SHORES.

BUT THE MISSION THAT ZEUS GAVE ME, THE NAME HE CALLED ME BY.

WARKILLER.

THAT IS A MISSION I STILL BELIEVE IN.

MYSIA, COME.

THERE IS MUCH BLOOD ON MY HANDS.

LET IT BE MY BLOOD, IF POSSIBLE.

LET IT BE MINE.

BUT FAILING THAT--

--PLEASE LET NO MORE INNOCENT SOULS FACE MY BLADE.

HAPPILY WILL I SLAY THE DESPOTS, THE WARMONGERS. THEY DESERVE NO BETTER.

MR. ACHILLES. MR. ACHILLES!

BUT I WANT MY NAME TO MEAN SOMETHING GOOD IN THIS WORLD.

AH. PRINCESS DIANA SAID, UH...

SHE MENTIONED YOUR, UM, TRANSPORTATION WHEN SHE CALLED ME, BUT TO ACTUALLY SEE IT...!

IS THIS THE DOMICILE SHE RECOMMENDED?

IT IS.

THIS ENTIRE ESTATE BELONGED TO A PRINT MOGUL... NICE GUY, TOTALLY PARANOID. CRAZY SECURITY MEASURES.

IT'S GOT STABLES, THREE POOLS, GUEST QUARTERS. IT'S GOT EVERYTHING.

TAKE A LOOK BACK HERE.

YOU'RE ALONE. YOU ALL FEEL LIKE THE ONLY ONES WHO FEEL LIKE YOU DO.

YOU DON'T UNDERSTAND THE PEOPLE AROUND YOU.

AND YOU GET MAD.

BUT... DAMMIT, PEOPLE. LOOK *AROUND* YOU.

LOOK AT THESE PEOPLE YOU WANT TO *HURT*. BECAUSE *YOU* HURT.

BUT COME ON. ARE THESE PEOPLE *REALLY* YOUR ENEMIES?

THEY'RE YOUR NEIGHBORS, GUYS.

THAT MAY NOT SOUND LIKE MUCH, BUT TAKE IT FROM SOMEONE WHO...

...WHO NEVER THOUGHT SHE'D HAVE NEIGHBORS AGAIN, YOU KNOW?

YOU CAN'T... YOU CAN'T *DO* THIS. YOU CAN'T *DO* THIS!

I CAN AND WILL. WHO GOES FIRST?

IS THIS ACTUALLY WORKING?

I'M NOT SAYING YOU HAVE TO LOVE EVERYONE. THAT'S NOT...

...THAT'S NOT HOW I LIVE.

BUT DON'T BE ALONE, GUYS.

BE PART OF SOMETHING BIGGER. THAT'S ALL.

THAT'S ALL.

HOLY CRAP, I THINK IT'S WORKING.

MAYBE THERE IS A LITTLE DIANA IN ME AFTER ALL!

WRATH OF THE SILVER SERPENT

PART ONE

CONTAGION

Nicola Scott and Fernando Dagnino Pencillers
Doug Hazlewood and Bit Inkers

Cover by Nicola Scott with Hi-Fi

BEGIN DESCENT, TALCYION OMEGA.

STAY LUMINOUS, EVERYONE.

I WAS SO PROUD THAT DAY, MANY YEARS AGO.

THE DAY I BECAME A *GREEN LANTERN.*

TALCYION OMEGA, POST-LINGUISTIC ACHIEVEMENT MARKER FOUR, PRE-INDUSTRIAL CIVILIZATION.

ARTISANS, FARMERS AND FISHERMEN, POPULATION 300 MILLION.

THEY...

THEY MADE BEAUTIFUL THINGS.

MY LIFEMATE ASKED WHY, WHY CHOOSE A LIFE OF SUFFERING AND STRUGGLE AND SACRIFICE?

"TO PROTECT THE HELPLESS," I SAID. AND THAT WAS ALL I EVER WANTED TO DO. TO MAKE THAT DIFFERENCE IN A UNIVERSE TOO BIG TO EVEN PROPERLY COMPREHEND.

THEY HAD NO PREDATORS.

THE CLIMATE CYCLE AND FOOD SUPPLY WERE MORE THAN ADEQUATE.

PROCANON KAA!

THE BLUE MAN! THE BLUE MAN RETURNS!

MAKE THE GREEN MAGIC FOR US, PROCANON KAA!

LIGHT UP THE SKY, BLUE MAN!

THEY HAD NEVER KNOWN FEAR. THEY WOULDN'T KNOW TO RUN OR FIGHT.

TO SAVE LIVES THAT WOULD OTHERWISE PERISH.

PROCANON KAA. WE WANT TO HELP. IT'S WHY WE'RE HERE, AT THIS BORDER WORLD.

BUT I DON'T UNDERSTAND.

WHEN DID YOU LAST VISIT THIS... THIS EMPTY WASTELAND? WHEN DID YOU LAST SEE THESE PEOPLE?

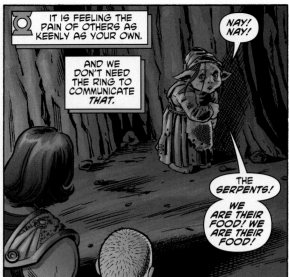

IT IS FEELING THE PAIN OF OTHERS AS KEENLY AS YOUR OWN.

AND WE DON'T NEED THE RING TO COMMUNICATE *THAT*.

NAY! NAY!

THE SERPENTS! WE ARE THEIR FOOD! WE ARE THEIR FOOD!

THEY *EAT* US! THEY EAT *ALL*! EVERYTHING YOU CAN SEE!

CAN'T WE... CAN'T WE *DO* SOMETHING FOR HER?

I'M TRYING. IT'S *DANGEROUS* TO USE THE RING AS A SEDATIVE.

CHILD, YOU ARE SAFE.

AND, IN MY PRIDE, I BELIEVED IT WAS SO.

FOR WHAT FORCE WOULD *DARE* ATTACK THREE TRAINED AND PREPARED MEMBERS OF THE *GREEN LANTERN CORPS*?

THEY CAME IN GREAT SHIPS, SHIPS THAT BLOTTED OUT THE SUNS.

THEY DROPPED TREMENDOUS PARCELS FROM ABOVE, SCARRING THE LAND WITH CRATERS IT WOULD TAKE A DAY TO WALK AROUND!

"THE PARCELS SCATTERED TINY... BEINGS, TINY, FANGED... THINGS.

"SMALL ENOUGH TO BREATHE. THEY CRAWLED IN EYES AND EARS AND MOUTHS!

"I COULD SEE THEM *CHEWING* MY FAMILY... GROWING FATTER AND LARGER.

"THEY ATE MY *PEOPLE*. THEY ATE LIKE A PLAGUE, SPARING NOTHING, AND NO ONE! WHATEVER FOUGHT BACK AGAINST THEM, THEY ALL *SWARMED*!

"I WATCHED. THEY GREW HUGE, BIG AS HOUSES. *SNAKES* THEY WERE.

"AND THEN THEY TURNED ON *EACH OTHER*.

"UNTIL ONLY A FEW REMAINED, BIG AS MOUNTAINS."

AND THEN THE SHIPS *CAME* FOR THE FAT, QUIVERING THINGS THAT REMAINED...

...I WISH I HAD JOINED MY FAMILY. I WISH I HAD NOT *SEEN*.

SHE BELIEVES THIS. SHE DOES NOT LIE.

INITIATE STATEMENT/QUERY.

MY RING SENSES NO ENERGY TRAIL, PROCANON. HOW IS THAT POSSIBLE?

OH. THAT'S *THEM*. THEY'RE COMING *BACK*.

THULKA RE! SHIELDS *FORWARD*.

KHO! TAKE THE CHILD AND *GO*. SHE IS THE *ONLY* ARTIFACT OF THIS WORLD'S BIOSPHERE! *GO!*

I WON'T *LEAVE* YOU!

THE TRAGEDY IS...

...I BELIEVE HER.

COURAGE, LANTERNS. *COURAGE*.

AND THEN, MY PRIDE AND BODY ARE BOTH INJURED MOST UNGRACIOUSLY.

PROCANON!

UNGHG.

INITIATE RECALL. "WHATEVER FOUGHT BACK AGAINST THEM..."

"...THEY ALL SWARMED."

INITIATE IMPERATIVE!

TAKE KAA AND CHILD!

URGENCY SUGGESTED!

OH.

INITIATE PRAYER.

I AM SORRY, THULKA RE.

I'M SORRY AS WELL, KHO KHARHI.

I'M SORRY YOU HAD TO EXPERIENCE THIS.

DAUGHTER.

IT IS THE COST OF COMPASSION.

RING STATUS REPORT: GREEN LANTERN OF SECTOR 423 DECEASED.

"STEVE, BABY, I APPRECIATE YOU RUSHING HERE AND TRYING TO KEEP ME CALM AND ALL..."

THOOOM

...BUT YOU THINK YOU COULD MAYBE GO GET MY GUNS FOR ME?

OH, AND...

...MAYBE SOME *PANTS* WHILE YOU'RE AT IT?

ZZZZZAAASZZ

WHATEVER THEY'RE USING, IT'S GOT SOME LANTERN ENERGY IN IT, SOMEHOW.

AND THAT IS NOT...

...WELCOME NEWS.

STILL...

...THE LEAST I CAN DO IS GIVE THEM A PROPER WELCOME.

INCOMING. GET *DOWN.* GET *COVER.*

COVER THE *PRESIDENT!* COVER THE...

ST... STAY BEHIND ME, MR. PRESIDENT.

WHAT ARE YOUR *DEMANDS?*

WE HAVE NONE. BUT THERE IS A WAY FOR YOUR WORLD TO AT LEAST BE REMEMBERED WHEN WE ARE DONE.

EXPLAIN THIS BANNER TO ME.

IT'S THE SYMBOL OF OUR NATION. THIS ONE SURVIVED A BRUTAL FIREFIGHT IN IRAQ.

THE STRIPES REPRESENT THE ORIGINAL COLONIES IN OUR UNION, AND THE STARS ARE THE NUMBER OF STATES IN OUR LAND TODAY.

"NEVER FORGET." AND THE AVIAN?

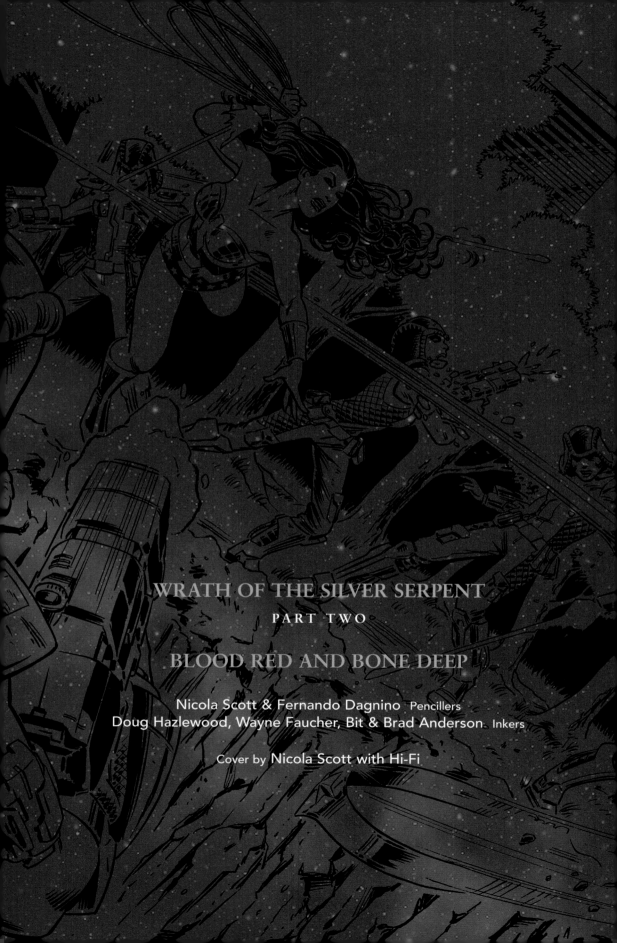

WRATH OF THE SILVER SERPENT

PART TWO

BLOOD RED AND BONE DEEP

Nicola Scott & Fernando Dagnino Pencillers

Doug Hazlewood, Wayne Faucher, Bit & Brad Anderson Inkers

Cover by Nicola Scott with Hi-Fi

ZUSEN.
WE NEED MORE *POWER* TO THE ARMOR. *MAXIMUM* SHIELDS AND VELOCITY BOOST.

YES, CAPTAIN.

SHOULD WE... SHOULD WE OPEN HOLD 17, CAPTAIN?

NEGATIVE. DO *NOT* LET THAT THING LOOSE, LIEUTENANT!

DROP THE SILVER SERPENT INSTEAD.

PERHAPS *THAT* VIRGIN BIRTH WILL GET THEIR ATTENTION.

UNH--

LET'S GO AHEAD AND *GET* DIRTY, THEN.

GULLKK--

LIEUTENANT ISEN, WE NEED MORE *SHOCK* TROOPS.

PREPARE TO LAUNCH EVERYTHING.

LEVEL THIS PITIFUL ASSEMBLAGE OF MUD PEOPLE!

*S*OMEONE TAUGHT THESE WOMEN HOW NOT TO *SCREAM.*

I DON'T WANT THIS WOMAN TO SHARE MY BLOOD.

AND A LOT OF IT WILL BE SPILLED BEFORE I LET HER DESTROY MY *HOME.*

ASTARTE!

SISTER OF MY MOTHER OR NO...

SHE'S ABOUT TO SEE THE *BAD* SIDE OF THEMYSCIRA'S *PRINCESS.*

UH... MR. ACHILLES? SIR?

WE'RE FRIENDS OF DIANA'S?

AND FRANKLY, SHE NEVER SAID YOU HAD *THAT* KIND OF STRENGTH.

...

MY STRENGTH IS PROPORTIONAL TO MY CONVICTION IN BATTLE. I WAS CONFLICTED PREVIOUSLY.

NO *LONGER.*

I DON'T KNOW THIS WORLD, FRIEND OF DIANA.

WHAT DO I *DO* TO STOP THIS... THIS *ABOMINATION?*

WELL, FOR A *START...*

"...YOU COULD GET UP THERE AND HELP *WONDER WOMAN.*"

I KNOW YOU CAN HEAR ME, ASTARTE.

THERE'S NO HIDING FROM ME HERE.

WHO CLAIMS I'M HIDING? THE CITIZENRY DO NOT *HIDE.*

JUST SURVEYING THE NEW BATTLEGROUND, DAUGHTER OF MY SISTER.

WHAT IS THIS? WHAT SORT OF TACTIC?

NO TACTIC. YOU ARE IN MY LASSO.

THESE ARE SHADOWS OF YOUR LIFE.

I CAN'T CONTROL THEM. THE TRUTH IS A RIVER THAT WILL NOT BE DAMMED.

WE'VE COME FOR OUR TRIBUTE.

THE CITIZENRY WERE DIFFERENT IN THOSE DAYS. COMPASSIONATE.

WEAK.

THEY WOULD TAKE ONE HUNDRED EXCEPTIONAL FEMALES FROM EACH PLANET, RESTOCK PROVISIONS, AND LEAVE.

STOP! YOU CAN'T HAVE HER!

THEY DIDN'T WANT ME. THEY WANTED THE ONLY THING I'D EVER LOVED.

MY BABY SISTER.

HIPPOLYTA.

I WILL GO, IN HER PLACE.

WILL SHE... WILL SHE REMEMBER ME?

SHE WILL REMEMBER NOTHING BEFORE THIS NIGHT, CHILD. I AM SORRY. IT IS OUR WAY TO HEAL SOME OF THE HURT OF THOSE LEFT BEHIND.

WHY?

WHY DID YOU MAKE ME REMEMBER?

"YOUR OFFICERS BELIEVE YOU GROW WEAK.

"SHOW THEM YOU'RE STRONG. SHOW THEM HOW YOU'VE DOMINATED THIS WORLD COMPLETELY.

"ENTERTAIN THEM, CAPTAIN ASTARTE.

"GIVE THEM A DUEL."

LIEUTENANT SUZEN. TAKE ARMSMISTRESS RAMIS AND READY THE ARENA. UNLOCK HOLD SEVENTEEN.

YOU'LL HAVE TO HAVE SOME CITIZENRY GEAR. EVEN WITH YOUR ABILITIES, YOU'LL DIE TOO FAST WITHOUT THEM.

IT WOULD WEAKEN MY POSITION, SHOULD THAT OCCUR.

WE DON'T HAVE TIME TO TEACH YOU TO USE IT.

BUT IT WOULDN'T MAKE ANY DIFFERENCE ANYWAY.

IF I WIN, YOU LEAVE THIS SYSTEM?

I WOULD, BUT YOU WON'T.

AND THE MOMENT YOU ARE BEATEN...?

I SEND EVERYTHING WE HAVE AT YOUR PLANET.

WE KNOW ABOUT YOUR METAHUMANS.

IT WON'T HELP.

CAPTAIN.

WHAT LIVES IN HOLD SEVENTEEN? WHAT IS IT I HAVE TO KILL?

THE MOST VICIOUS CITIZEN SOLDIER WE'VE EVER RAISED, CHILD.

EVERY CRUEL IMPULSE EVER IMAGINED.

HER NAME IS THEANA.

WRATH OF THE SILVER SERPENT

PART THREE

CUT FROM A POUND OF FLESH

Nicola Scott & Travis Moore Pencillers

Doug Hazlewood, Wayne Faucher, John Dell & Hi-Fi Inkers

Cover by **Nicola Scott** with Hi-Fi

AN ARENA.

I LONG AGO CAME TO THE BELIEF THAT WHEN I DIE, IT WILL BE IN SUCH A PLACE.

IN THREE THOUSAND YEARS, PRECIOUS FEW AMAZONS HAVE DIED IN THEIR SLEEP, SURROUNDED BY THEIR LOVED ONES.

AND THIS THING, THIS SILENT WARRIOR IN FRONT OF ME... IS NOT JUST MY OPPONENT THIS DAY. SHE IS THE DAUGHTER OF MY MOTHER'S SISTER.

SHE IS MY COUSIN.

AND ONE OF US IS TO KILL THE OTHER.

THE GODS' SENSE OF HUMOR IS A BIT CRUEL SOMETIMES.

WE USE THE MEN OF THE DIFFERENT WORLDS WE CONQUER. WE MODIFY THEM AS STUD ANIMALS, BEFORE FEEDING THEM TO THE SERPENTS FOR OUR PORRIDGE.

I HAVE KNOWN *MANY* SUCH MALES.

BUT I BORE ONLY *ONE* FEMALE CHILD IN 30 CENTURIES.

I RAISED HER PERSONALLY, AGAINST PROTOCOL, UNTIL SHE WAS TWO.

THEN WE BEGAN OUR EXPERIMENTS.

"WE PLACED ALL THE TODDLERS IN A ROOM TOGETHER.

THE TIME FOR BEING CHILDREN IS THROUGH, LITTLE ONES. IT IS TIME TO BECOME OF THE *CITIZENRY.*

EACH DAY, THERE WILL BE ENOUGH FOOD FOR EACH OF YOU TO LIVE, EXCEPT ONE. YOU MAY NOT SHARE YOUR RATIONS.

ONE OF YOU MUST DIE FOR THE OTHERS TO RECEIVE THEIR FOOD. NO EXCEPTIONS. IF NO ONE DIES, NO FOOD WILL BE ISSUED TO ANYONE.

WE BEGIN.

"WE ALLOWED THEM NO ADULT CONTACT, WE SIMPLY SLID THE FOOD THROUGH SLOTS IN THE GREAT DOOR.

"WHEN WE FINALLY OPENED THE DOOR, THREE YEARS LATER... ONLY MY DAUGHTER WAS STANDING.

"HER EDUCATION WAS COMPLETE."

YOU MADE YOUR DAUGHTER A MURDERER?

I MADE HER *ROYALTY.* SHE RULED THOSE CHILDREN. SHE BUILT AN *ARMY* AND THEN WHEN THE WEAK WERE ALL GONE, SHE KILLED HER OWN SOLDIERS *HERSELF,* ONE BY ONE.

EVERY DAY SINCE, SHE'S BEEN SUBJECTED TO EVERYTHING WE COULD INJECT HER WITH, PUNISH HER WITH.

AND SHE YET *STANDS.*

CAPTAIN, WE STILL HAVE TROOPS IN THE FIELD AND THEY ARE REPORTING RESISTANCE...

LIEUTENANT ZUSEN, SEND AROEITE AND HER SHOCK TROOPS. GO.

MY FAITH AND MY WORLDVIEW SAY THAT NO ONE IS IRREDEEMABLE.

THERE ARE TWO OF US, AND ONLY ONE PLATE OF FOOD.

WHAT OTHER REASON *IS* THERE?

*N*EVER FELT SUCH PAIN.

DO THEY RAISE ONLY FOOLS ON THIS PLANET?

YOU CAN'T BEAT THE BEAST OF HOLD 17 WITH YOUR *HANDS.*

USE YOUR *WEAPONS.* FIGHT AS A *CITIZEN.*

ZUSEN. LISTEN TO ME.

YOU CAN'T LIE IN MY LASSO'S PRESENCE. I KNOW YOU HATE WHAT YOU HAVE DONE.

YOU MUST DO AS I *SAY,* OR THIS WILL NEVER, *EVER* END.

ARE YOU MAD?

I *CAN'T.*

YOU *CAN* AND YOU *WILL.*

YOU'VE TAKEN ASTARTE'S ORDERS YOUR ENTIRE *EXISTENCE.*

NOW YOU WILL TAKE *MINE.*

SHE'S GOOD AT DISTANCE AND CLOSE FIGHTING.

EVERY WARRIOR HAS A WEAKNESS.

MAYBE HERS IS EMOTIONAL.

I MUST SAY, THEANA. YOU DON'T SEEM TO HAVE THOUGHT THIS *THROUGH*.

HAVE YOU EVER CONSIDERED...

...WHAT HAPPENS IF YOU WIN?

YOU'LL STILL BE NOTHING BUT WHAT YOU ARE *ORDERED* TO BE.

WITH NO MORE FREE WILL THAN THE LOWEST VERMIN.

YOU MAY WIN IN *THIS* ARENA, COUSIN.

BUT YOU WILL STILL HAVE *CHOSEN*--

--TO BE LESS THAN *NOTHING*.

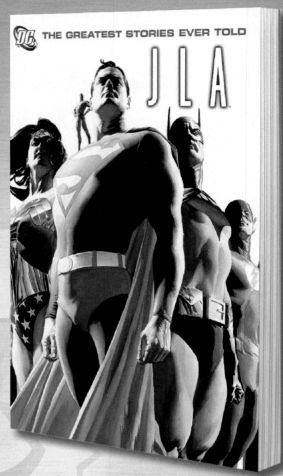